AF208209

JESUS IS

JESUS IS

A 31-DAY DEVOTIONAL ON THE "I AM" STATEMENTS OF JESUS

The door of the sheep · The good shepherd · The resurrection and the life · the truth, and the life · The true vine · The bread of life · The light of the world

DR. BRYAN GILL

PUBLISHED BY

IRON HILL

press

MY FAITH RESTS NOT UPON WHAT I AM,
OR SHALL BE,
OR FEEL,
OR KNOW,
BUT IN WHAT CHRIST IS,
IN WHAT HE HAS DONE,
AND IN WHAT HE IS NOW DOING FOR ME.

CHARLES SPURGEON

CONTENTS

INTRODUCTION

I am thrilled that you are beginning this 31-day journey through the seven "I am" statements of Jesus found in the Book of John. When I started brainstorming about writing a new devotional book, I had you in mind. I wanted to create a meaningful devotional experience rich with Scripture and careful exegesis while at the same time providing practical application. The world doesn't need more fluff—the world needs more of Jesus. And what better way to help you understand Jesus more fully than to study Him using the words He used to describe Himself.

If you are unfamiliar with the significance of Jesus' "I am" statements, you probably have a few questions. Like, why are these statements important? What do they mean for believers? Why write a book about them? It's difficult to overstate the importance of what Jesus was doing when He made these declarations. When Jesus said, "I am," He was making a bold statement about His identity: "In using the expression, Jesus seems to be explicitly identifying Himself with Yahweh, asserting His eternality, self-existence, and changelessness, and claiming to bear Yahweh's presence on Earth."[1] Studying these "I am" statements is extremely beneficial to Christ-followers as it unlocks a deeper understanding of Jesus' identity.

In the book of John, Jesus says the statement, "I am the…" seven different times. Below are the statements and where they appear in John's Gospel.

1. I am the bread of life. (John 6:35)
2. I am the light of the world. (John 8:12)
3. I am the door. (John 10:7)
4. I am the good shepherd. (John 10:11)
5. I am the resurrection and the life. (John 11:25)
6. I am the way, and the truth, and the life. (John 14:6)
7. I am the true vine. (John 15:1)

Each of these statements tells us something about the character and purpose of Jesus. Over the next 31 days, we will dive deeper into these seven statements from a historical and personal perspective. In a sense, these are seven divine metaphors that Jesus used to help illustrate points He was trying to make. Jesus, being a masterful teacher, communicated difficult concepts through imagery. However, some imagery is lost on us since we live in a Westernized culture in the twenty-first century. My hope for us over the next 31 days is that we can reclaim some of the intent behind what Jesus wanted the original hearers to understand when He made these statements.

Just as a fair warning, this devotional isn't full of stories and illustrations. While some are sprinkled throughout, I wanted to focus more on the theology and message of what Scripture is saying. I hope you will find this a rich and robust approach to your daily devotional time as we look at the Old and New Testaments to better grasp what Jesus meant with these seven statements.

Now, you may ask yourself, if there are only seven statements, what will fill up the rest of the days? I'm glad you asked. Each of the seven statements gets a day dedicated to introducing the statement and its context. The days following will help us look at Bible passages related to each "I am" statement. Looking at other verses and passages of Scripture will help us unlock some of the mystery behind what Jesus wanted His original audience to hear and help us apply these truths to our lives.

I am thankful for you and encouraged that you are intentionally growing closer to Jesus. I am honored that this book can be a small part of what God is doing in your life. I pray that, once you complete this book, you will better understand Jesus as our Savior and why He is the only one who could be worthy of forgiving us of our sins and drawing us into the full life He promises in His Word.

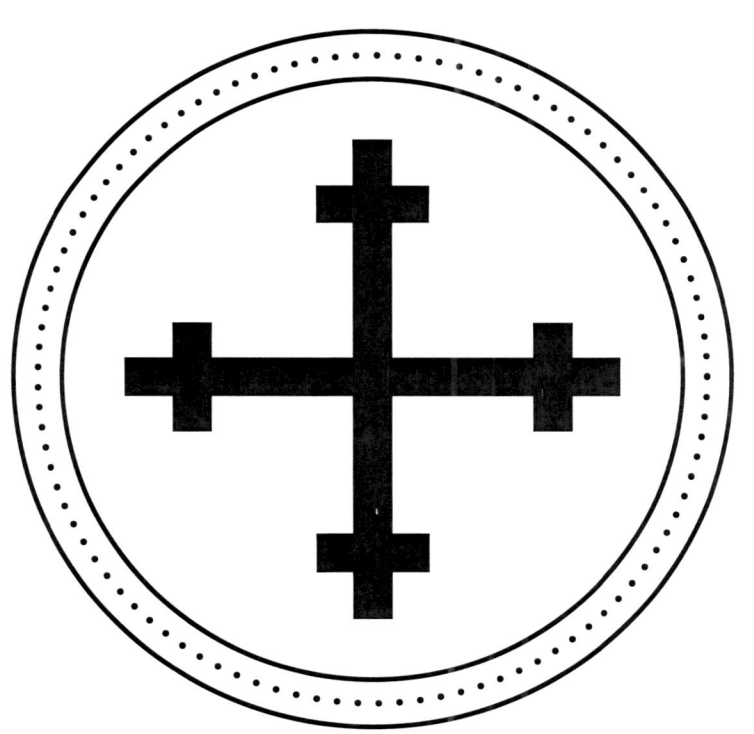

DAY 1
THE BREAD OF LIFE

Jesus said to them, "I am the bread of life; whoever comes to me shall not hunger, and whoever believes in me shall never thirst." - John 6:35

For thousands of years, having bread has meant security, stability, nourishment, and provision. The year 2020 was a big year for bread-making. The world was in turmoil, and many people decided to make bread. Traffic to bread-making websites skyrocketed above their normal engagement levels, social media channels were filled with bread-making tutorials, and yeast products flew off the shelves. For most, baking bread not only provided a great distraction but meant that their nutritional needs would be met even if they couldn't reach the grocery store. In the south, when the weatherman says it's going to snow, people rush to the store to stock up on bread and milk and hunker down. Historically, bread was one of the first foods that didn't involve hunting or gathering. It meant that a wheat crop was plentiful, and provisions and time were adequate to make bread.

When I think about the miracles of Jesus, two come to mind: Jesus feeding the five thousand with fish and bread and Jesus walking on water. These two have been my favorites since my early days of Sunday school and vacation Bible school. According to the Gospel of John, they happened on the same day—one right after the other. Jesus fed the crowd with a little boy's sack lunch and then went off by Himself to pray. Later that night, as the disciples had traveled several miles out onto the sea, Jesus caught up with them by walking on the water. What a wild night!

The next day, some of the same people from the crowd He'd fed the day before were hanging around to try to catch Jesus again. They found Him on the other side of the sea and demanded to see more signs. They started asking questions and equating Jesus' bread and fish miracle to the Israelites being given manna in the desert. Jesus quickly told them that all those Israelites died, but He was the bread of life and offered eternal life to those who believed in Him. As you can imagine, that completely confused them (we will dive into this more in this week's devotions).

When I think about the statement, "I am the bread of life," I can't help but think about all the things that bread represented for Jesus' original audience. For many, this image of security came to mind because they had just been fed in their time of need the day before. For others, the thought of bread baking in their home as that sweet aroma wafted through the air evoked a feeling of nostalgia and stability. Still others thought about God's provision to their ancestors in the desert through manna from heaven. As we will see in this chapter, Jesus, being the bread of life, meant that He was all of these: security, stability, nourishment, and provision.

This prayer is from the Book of Common Prayer and is typically used on the fourth Sunday of Lent. Pray it now as we begin this chapter into Jesus' statement, "I am the bread of life."

GRACIOUS FATHER,
WHOSE BLESSED SON JESUS CHRIST
CAME DOWN FROM HEAVEN
TO BE THE TRUE BREAD
WHICH GIVES LIFE TO THE WORLD:

EVERMORE GIVE US THIS BREAD,
THAT HE MAY LIVE IN US, AND WE IN HIM;
WHO LIVES AND REIGNS WITH YOU
AND THE HOLY SPIRIT,
ONE GOD, NOW AND FOREVER.
AMEN.

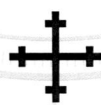

DAY 2
THE BREAD OF LIFE

Then the LORD said to Moses, "Behold, I am about to rain bread from heaven for you, and the people shall go out and gather a day's portion every day, that I may test them, whether they will walk in my law or not." - Exodus 16:4

The Israelites were notorious for complaining, especially after God had just done something amazing to deliver them from some type of danger. In this instance, God delivered them out of Egypt, where they had been enslaved for hundreds of years. However, that wasn't good enough. They didn't see the opportunity of becoming a nation of their own out from under the rule of the Pharoah. Only a month into their journey, they were focused on their problems and their hunger rather than their deliverance from bondage. They would've rather died in Egypt with full bellies than live free and hungry. Completely ungrateful, they complained about their food situation to Moses and Aaron.

But what did God do? He provided for His people despite their ungratefulness. God gave Moses and Aaron specific instructions for the Israelites, and each morning, as the dew dried on the ground around their tents, a strange flat bread-like substance had formed on the ground that they called manna. And each day, everyone gathered as much as they needed, some more than others, and it never ran out. The next day, God did it all over again. And each day after that as well. As long as they were in the wilderness until they reached the Promised Land, God provided bread from heaven to meet their needs.

This bread from heaven was symbolic of God's sustaining grace for His people. This story beautifully illustrates God's goodness and graciousness despite our actions. His grace never runs out. Some of us need more than others, but God never tires of giving good gifts to His children. Like Jeremiah wrote in Lamentations 3:22–24, "The steadfast love of the LORD never ceases; his mercies never come to an end; they are new every morning; great is your faithfulness. 'The LORD is my portion,' says my soul, 'therefore I will hope in him.'"

God's provision for His people was not proportionate to their obedience, and God's grace to us is not determined by our performance. We need Jesus, and no amount of work can earn the grace He freely gives.

When Jesus said, "I am the bread of life," He was saying that His love never runs out, His grace never runs out, and every day, like bread from heaven, your soul will no longer be hungry because it will be satisfied in Him.

QUESTIONS

1. In what areas of your life can you show more gratitude toward God today?

2. What can you start doing each day that would acknowledge the goodness of God and that will remind you that His love never fails?

3. Take a moment to pray and thank God for His provision and new mercies each day.

DAY 3
THE BREAD OF LIFE

But you, O Bethlehem Ephrathah, who are too little to be among the clans of Judah, from you shall come forth for me one who is to be ruler in Israel, whose coming forth is from of old, from ancient days. - Micah 5:2

Words are important in the Bible. People's names have meaning, and we often see that names of places also have meaning. As you may know, the Old Testament was written in Hebrew, and the New Testament was written in Greek. To the original hearers and readers of Scripture, the words used for names and places were easily recognized, and they understood the meaning behind these nouns. However, for us in the twenty-first century who do not speak the biblical languages, we must do a little more digging.

It has been said that people have an "aha" moment when learning a foreign language. They're studying along, and suddenly, the words and sentence structures begin to make sense, and they begin to comprehend the foreign language just as well as their native tongue. Full transparency: When I was in Hebrew class in seminary, that "aha" moment never came. But, one class stood out to me—the one where we learned what the name "Bethlehem" meant.

Bethlehem was a small and unimportant city compared to the other places in Judah. But, long before Jesus, several recognizable characters were associated with this little town in one way or another: Ruth, Boaz, Samuel, and David, to name a few. The word Bethlehem is made up of two words: beth and lehem. Beth means "house," and lehem means "bread." Therefore, Bethlehem literally means "house of bread." To the Israelites that came before Jesus, Bethlehem's name wasn't very significant. But Jesus changes everything.

God historically uses the unassuming, weak, and undersized to accomplish His purposes. Think about an old man named Abraham with a barren wife being the parents to a nation. Or about David defeating Goliath or Gideon and the 300 soldiers. Or about the mighty walls of Jericho falling after the Israelites walked around the city and blew horns. Paul said it best in 1 Corinthians 1:27: "But God chose what is foolish in the world to shame the wise; God chose what is weak in the world to shame the strong."

It was no coincidence that God chose Bethlehem as the birthplace of Jesus; He was making a statement that He could do great things with the unlikeliest places and people. So, when Jesus, born in the "house of bread," claimed He was "the bread of life," it all started to make sense. This claim was prophetic and pointed to God's greater purpose for all people. Because of Jesus, we know about a little town called Bethlehem. If you think your life doesn't have meaning, think about what Jesus can do with you. Jesus changes everything.

QUESTIONS

1. What do you think gives people purpose in life? Is it their money? Their job? Their status?

2. Describe a time when you felt like your life had no meaning. How did you come out of this time?

3. If you trust Jesus with your life, you will always have a purpose, no matter how small you think that purpose is. Pray for God to remind you each day that because of Jesus, you are important.

DAY 4
THE BREAD OF LIFE

But he answered, "It is written, "'Man shall not live by bread alone, but by every word that comes from the mouth of God.'" - Matthew 4:1-4

You may have read this passage before and might be familiar with what is happening here. But let's be honest, this is a wild story. Jesus is just coming off a forty-day fast in the wilderness, and the devil shows up to tempt Him. I love this story because it shows Jesus' humanity. I think sometimes we forget that Jesus was fully human and fully God. This passage points out that Jesus was hungry. This allows us to relate to Jesus in His humanity because we all know what hunger is like. Your body aches, your stomach growls, you can't think clearly, your muscles are weak, your mouth is dry, and all you want in life is sustenance to quench the hunger. That was the same feeling Jesus had after fasting for forty days. Then look who shows up.

Isn't it like the devil to show up when we are weakest? He knew his inferiority to Jesus and thought he could catch Jesus off guard. However, when we are at our weakest and fully dependent on the supernatural power of God's Holy Spirit, we are actually at our strongest. As Paul said in 2 Corinthians 12:10, "For when I am weak, then I am strong."

When the devil tempted Jesus to turn the rocks into bread to satisfy His hunger, I imagine a smirk coming over Jesus' face as He thought back to the Israelites in the desert receiving bread from heaven, back where He was born, and then to the future when He would soon claim that "I am the bread of life." Then, I love how Jesus responds. He quotes Scripture, a passage from Deuteronomy 8:3.

This passage in Deuteronomy was a reminder that just as the bread that fell from heaven in the desert was temporary fulfillment, the bread that the devil offered was also a temporary fix. Jesus was familiar with this scheme and reminded the devil that while bread is temporary, the Word of God is eternal, and when we live by the Word of God, we have true life. One quick takeaway here is when the devil tempts each of us, the only appropriate response and our only defense is the Word of God.

But let's not confuse the phrase "every word that comes from the mouth of God," to be limited to the Scriptures and exclude the person of Jesus. John 1 states, "In the beginning was the Word, and the Word was with God, and the Word was God. … And the Word became flesh and dwelt among us, and we have seen his glory, glory as of the only Son from the Father, full of grace and truth." You see, Jesus is talking about Himself when He quotes the Deuteronomy passage because He was the fulfillment of this passage as the Word that became flesh. When Jesus states, "I am the bread of life; whoever comes to me shall not hunger, and whoever believes in me shall never thirst," He claims that He can satisfy your physical and spiritual needs.

QUESTIONS

1. What "rocks" does the devil try to tempt you with?

2. What does Jesus want you to replace the temporary fulfillment of "rocks" with?

3. In what ways can you begin to live on the Word of God? What does that look like in your life starting today?

DAY 5
THE BREAD OF LIFE

Give us this day our daily bread. - Matthew 6:11

This passage is a snippet from when Jesus was teaching His disciples how to pray. I'm afraid that many of us reading this gloss over this simple sentence because we don't worry about daily food. If we need food or bread, we log on to our food delivery app or go to the nearest grocery store and get what we want. However, nearly 193 million people worldwide do not know where their next meal is coming from.[2] When you have food insecurity, this prayer means more. It means complete reliance on God's provision for our needs each day. For many of us, our relative affluence puts us at a disadvantage in fully understanding this prayer. But Jesus teaches us to pray in this way so that we will never forget that God is our provider, and regardless of our status or wealth, we must rely on Him daily.

In addition to the provision of physical daily bread, scholars believe this passage also has an eschatological meaning. Eschatology is the study of end times. When we read this verse, "Give us today our daily bread," through the lens of what happens to our souls when we die, we also see God as not only the sustainer of us here on earth with physical food but also the sustainer of our souls for eternity. The prayer has a double meaning that relies on God to provide today's portion of bread and tomorrow's portion in eternity.

After Jesus proclaimed, "I am the bread of life," He further explains His purpose on earth. He states, "For I have come down from heaven, not to do my own will but the will of him who sent me. And this is the will of him who sent me, that I should lose nothing of all that he has given me, but raise it up on the last day. For this is the will of my Father, that everyone who looks on the Son and believes in him should have eternal life, and I will raise him up on the last day" (John 6:38–40).

When we pray, "Give us today our daily bread," we should put ourselves in a posture of pleading with God to sustain us now and forever. To get into that right alignment, we must see through the lie that we are in control and can sustain ourselves by our job or bank account because it can all go away instantly. In Philippians 4:12–13, the Apostle Paul reminds us of this: "I know how to be brought low, and I know how to abound. In any and every circumstance, I have learned the secret of facing plenty and hunger, abundance and need. I can do all things through him who strengthens me." I hate to break it to us, but this passage isn't about sports and weightlifting. It's about fully relying on God here today and tomorrow for eternity.

QUESTIONS

1. In what ways are you trusting in your strength for provision? Think about this for a moment and be as specific as you can.

2. Your job, vehicles, and house all come from God. How can you remind yourself daily that all provision comes from the Lord?

3. Pray now that God will give you a spirit of contentment with what He provides. Pray that you will not desire another person's portion and will be satisfied with what God gives you, whether much or little.

DAY 6
THE BREAD OF LIFE

And he took bread, and when he had given thanks, he broke it and gave it to them, saying, "This is my body, which is given for you. Do this in remembrance of me." - Luke 22:19

Pyotr Ilyich Tchaikovsky was a Russian composer who lived from 1840–1893. He composed symphonies such as The Nutcracker and Swan Lake, but my favorite Tchaikovsky piece is the 1812 Overture. It's Tchaikovsky's commemoration of Russia's victory over Napoleon and France in the French invasion of Russia in 1812. I would highly recommend it if you've never listened to this piece. It's an absolute masterpiece. It begins softly with flutes and violins, and over the next sixteen minutes, it continually builds from the gentle sounds of a peaceful time to what sounds like an oncoming train and ends with this incredible crescendo of trumpets, church bells, and actual cannon blasts. You can feel the pride in every note and almost see the victory flag being raised at the end. Give it a listen.

I feel like the Last Supper is similar in this way. When we look back to all the times God used bread in the centuries before Jesus, we see a continual building upon this theme. Jesus as the Bread of Life is the fulfillment of security, stability, nourishment, and provision as seen throughout Scripture. Building and building and getting louder and louder, the disciples begin to understand that Jesus is everything He said He was. Then, in a glorious crescendo, in the intimacy of the upper room, on the night before He was crucified, Jesus invited His followers to eat the bread that symbolized His body given to them.

I try to imagine the taste of that bread as if I were a disciple in the room. Would I have been brought to tears as I felt the crunch between my jaws? Would I have been enraged? Would I have been confused? I don't know. But I feel that although the disciples got it wrong on so many accounts and never fully understood until after Pentecost, they realized then what Jesus' claim of being the Bread of Life meant. For Jesus to be our security, stability, nourishment, and provision in this life and the afterlife, He would have to die. Paul explained in 1 Thessalonians 5:10 that Jesus "died for us so that whether we are awake or asleep we might live with him."

While I don't know what the disciples thoughts were as they ate the bread during that supper, I'm certain they were not the same people the next time they broke bread together. In the same way, when we eat the bread and drink the wine as a commemoration of Christ's victory over death and assurance of salvation for our souls, we should think of God's provision in the desert, Jesus' triumph over temptation, His daily sustenance in this life, and His promise of eternal life. Jesus is truly the Bread of Life.

QUESTIONS

1. Take a minute to reflect on your life and recognize the hand of God at work. Give an example of God's provision for you as a child.

2. Give an example of God's provision for you as a teenager.

3. Give an example of God's provision for you as an adult.

Take a minute to pray and thank God for His powerful and loving provision over your life.

DAY 7
THE LIGHT OF THE WORLD

Again Jesus spoke to them, saying, "I am the light of the world. Whoever follows me will not walk in darkness, but will have the light of life." - John 8:12

Light is vital for life. We benefit from sunshine on our skin because the ultraviolet rays help form Vitamin D in our body. Plants need light for photosynthesis to occur so that they will grow. Exposure to sunlight helps serotonin production, a chemical in the brain that helps fight depression. Light provides warmth to the body through the heat produced from the light. Light helps us see obstacles that could cause harm if we were to otherwise stumble over them in the dark. Without light, life would not exist. But even considering all that we know about light and its benefits, for the first-century hearers of Jesus' proclamation in John 8:12, light meant so much more.

When we want light today, we simply navigate to the flashlight app on our phone, flip a switch on the wall, or look to the nearest streetlight by our house. When Jesus' original audience heard Jesus say that He was "the light of the world," that meant that Jesus would provide safety, protection, and guidance. As people followed Jesus, they would not be subject to the obstacles that might ensnare those left in the dark. It meant that Jesus would help them see the path before them and that He would provide a way to avoid the dangerous entrapments that could cause them harm.

I'm an outdoorsman. And whether hunting, hiking, or early morning fishing, having some type of light helps. It helps to show where to step along the path, illuminate potential dangers on the trail, and identify hazardous distractions along the way.

Jesus' proclamation of Himself as "the light of the world" comes right after His interaction with the woman caught in adultery. Recall in John 8:1-11 that Jesus told the woman caught in adultery to "go and sin no more." While we are not sure when these two events took place in relation to each other, it is not far-fetched to think that they are related in intent and purpose. When Jesus said that He was the light of the world, and those who follow Him would not walk in darkness, it means that He will illuminate our path and we will be able to avoid the obstacles of this world, including the sins this woman caught in adultery had committed.

When Jesus is our light, we are able to see the things in our life that are dangerous to our walk with Christ and hazardous to our families. He helps illuminate the distractions that hinder us from becoming more like Him. Jesus' light shows us the straight path: "Trust in the LORD with all your heart, and do not lean on your own understanding. In all your ways acknowledge him, and he will make straight your paths" (Proverbs 3:5–6). When we lean on our own understanding, our paths will continue to be crooked. When we trust in Jesus, the Light, then He will illuminate the right, straight path.

This prayer is by Saint Francis of Assisi, a Catholic friar who was known for his care for the poor and underprivileged. Pray this prayer as you prepare your heart for the week ahead.

LORD, MAKE ME AN INSTRUMENT OF YOUR PEACE:

WHERE THERE IS HATRED, LET ME SOW LOVE;

WHERE THERE IS INJURY, PARDON;

WHERE THERE IS DOUBT, FAITH;

WHERE THERE IS DESPAIR, HOPE;

WHERE THERE IS DARKNESS, LIGHT;

WHERE THERE IS SADNESS, JOY.

O DIVINE MASTER, GRANT THAT I MAY NOT SO MUCH SEEK

TO BE CONSOLED AS TO CONSOLE,

TO BE UNDERSTOOD AS TO UNDERSTAND,

TO BE LOVED AS TO LOVE.

FOR IT IS IN GIVING THAT WE RECEIVE,

IT IS IN PARDONING THAT WE ARE PARDONED,

AND IT IS IN DYING THAT WE ARE BORN TO ETERNAL LIFE.

AMEN.

DAY 8
THE LIGHT OF THE WORLD

And God said, "Let there be light," and there was light. And God saw that the light was good. And God separated the light from the darkness. God called the light Day, and the darkness he called Night. And there was evening and there was morning, the first day. - Genesis 1:3-5

Light makes other things visible. Without light, everything would be dark. However, darkness is defined by the absence of light. We know darkness because there is something missing: light.

In the beginning, there was darkness. That meant that there was no light. Then, the Triune God spoke light into existence, and there was light. Creation could now be seen because of this light shining into the darkness.

Before Jesus' earthly ministry, this Genesis passage could've been viewed as simply a history lesson. Obviously, no one was there to witness this cosmic event, so it is by God's revelation to Moses that we have the written historical account of God as creator of the universe. However, now that we are on the other side of Jesus and His proclamation as the "light of the world," this opening passage of the Bible takes on a different meaning that goes far beyond simple history.

When we look at what Jesus did in the thirty-something years He walked this earth, we see that He was just continuing to do what He had always been doing: bringing light into the dark world. Jesus existed before His earthly birth as a baby in the manger. He was with God in the beginning, and through Him all things were made (John 1:1-3). As God, Jesus spoke light into existence. In the same way, Jesus Himself brought His light into a dark world. It is because of Jesus that we know what love is. As sinful people with dark hearts, we don't have to be shown how to be selfish and cruel; those come naturally. What we do need is to be shown how to love our neighbors and serve one another so that the light of Christ can be seen by the dark world.

God defeated the darkness by His word. In the same way, the only way we can defeat the darkness in our hearts is by God's Word. Hebrews 4:12 says, "For the word of God is living and active, sharper than any two-edged sword, piercing to the division of soul and of spirit, of joints and of marrow, and discerning the thoughts and intentions of the heart." When we have Jesus, we have to search ourselves and find those dark places that exist in the crevasses of our heart so that the light of Jesus can expose them. Then and only then can we grow to be more like Him.

QUESTIONS

1. If we are to search our hearts for these dark places, we need to humble ourselves and recognize that there are areas of our life that need to be exposed. Pray now that God would humble you and show you the dark places.

2. Write down 3-4 Bible verses you need to remind yourself of daily to defeat the dark corners of your heart.

DAY 9
THE LIGHT OF THE WORLD

Your word is a lamp to my feet and a light to my path. - Psalm 119:105

The only thing worse than having no flashlight in the dark woods is having a flashlight and not using it. I experienced this on a hunting trip not long ago. I was in an unfamiliar place and wanted to stay in the tree stand as long as I could. However, when the sun went down and the woods grew dark, I realized I had forgotten my flashlight—or so I thought. I lowered my rifle and gathered my things and started out on what I thought was the trail I'd traveled in on. Needless to say, I tripped over every root, vine, and briar in the woods. All because I didn't have a flashlight. It wasn't until I got back to the truck that I realized I had put my flashlight in one of my cargo pockets and not where I normally kept it.

Even though I had the light with me all along, it didn't do any good because I didn't use it.

If we read the verses prior to Psalm 119:105, we see that verses 97-104 are speaking about the different ways the Psalmist uses God's Word. God's Word makes him wise, gives him insight, keeps him away from evil, and brings him delight. Then, in verse 105, we see him refer to God's Word as a lamp to his feet and a light to his path. It is when the Psalmist uses God's Word and puts it into practice that his path is well lit. Simply knowing about God's Word and failing to practice it will not illuminate your path. James 1:22 says, "But be doers of the word, and not hearers only, deceiving yourselves."

When Jesus says that He is "the light of the world," He is offering so much more than we can imagine. He's offering wisdom, insight, and understanding. He's offering a way for you and me to stay away from evil. And He's inviting you to delight in Him and see what the true good life is all about.

There is a well-lit path marked out for you if you are willing to follow Jesus. But you can't just expect the path to show up if you are sporadically attending church, only reading God's Word on occasion, and your prayer life is limited to saying the blessing around the dinner table. You must live in God's Word and do what it says. Otherwise, it's like having a flashlight in the dark woods but never using it.

QUESTIONS

1. What ways can you put God's Word to use in your life today? Take the time to list these down. It will help you be more likely to put them into practice.

2. What do you think God will provide when you use His Word as a light to your path?

3. How will your life be different when God's Word guides you?

DAY 10
THE LIGHT OF THE WORLD

The people who walked in darkness have seen a great light; those who dwelt in a land of deep darkness, on them has light shone. - Isaiah 9:2

In writing, there is a moment when the protagonist, or main character, has lost all hope. This is called, "the dark night of the soul." The protagonist has done everything they could do to get out of the difficult situation, and nothing has worked. Everything they've tried has failed and there is no way out. All hope is lost. In novels and in movies, this is the moment of the story that holds the most tension. I'm sure you can think of the dark night of the soul moment in your favorite movie or book. However, while this is a tense scene, this is also where the best parts take place. This is where the hero or heroine steps in and saves the day.

When we back up a little from our key verse for today's devotional and read Isaiah 8:19-22, we see God's people in their dark night of the soul moment. They are described as distressed, hungry, enraged, in anguish, and lost. Wow. It doesn't get much darker than that. But what Isaiah says next is the best news of all.

In chapter 9, the tone shifts from hopelessness to hopefulness all because of what? A great light. That light that would save those who were walking in darkness was the prophecy of Jesus, our Savior. We know this because at the end of this chapter in verses 6-7, one of the greatest and most recognizable passages foretelling the coming of Jesus was written:

"[6] For to us a child is born, to us a son is given; and the government shall be upon his shoulder, and his name shall be called Wonderful Counselor, Mighty God, Everlasting Father, Prince of Peace. [7] Of the increase of his government and of peace there will be no end, on the throne of David and over his kingdom, to establish it and to uphold it with justice and with righteousness from this time forth and forevermore. The zeal of the LORD of hosts will do this."

When Jesus proclaimed that He was the light of the world, He was offering hope that would rescue you from your darkest moments, from the pit of despair, from the dark night of your soul for now and for eternity. He was reassuring us that He was indeed the fulfillment of this prophecy, the light that would deliver us from despair and darkness. And all we have to do is trust Him and submit to His authority. There is no other way, there is no other hope in this deep dark world. The only hope is Jesus.

QUESTIONS

1. When was a time when you felt that you were in the dark night of your soul?

2. How did God rescue you from your despair in your deepest time of need?

3. Because of this, what ways can you help others see that Jesus is their only hope in times of despair?

DAY 11
THE LIGHT OF THE WORLD

This is the message we have heard from him and proclaim to you, that God is light, and in him is no darkness at all. If we say we have fellowship with him while we walk in darkness, we lie and do not practice the truth. But if we walk in the light, as he is in the light, we have fellowship with one another, and the blood of Jesus his Son cleanses us from all sin. - 1 John 1:5-7

When you see someone in a uniform, certain things come to mind that define that person. If you see someone in scrubs, you automatically think they are in the healthcare industry and that they help people. If you see someone in a fireman's uniform, there's a level of bravery and character that person possesses that matches their profession. If someone is wearing a military uniform, you might think that there is a level of selflessness and toughness that that person has. However, when these people act outside of the expected attributes that accompany what their uniform represents, it's difficult for our minds to reconcile their behavior.

In the same way, if we claim to be followers of Jesus, but our actions do not reflect the light and love of God, we are still walking in darkness. Brennan Manning, author of The Ragamuffin Gospel said, "The greatest single cause of atheism in the world today is Christians who acknowledge Jesus with their lips, then walk out the door and deny him by their lifestyle. That is what an unbelieving world simply finds unbelievable."

The light of God affects our actions. Someone who is walking in the light of God will treat people differently, love others selflessly, and live as one who is forgiven. As believers, our actions will be countercultural when we're in business meetings. Our language will be kind and encouraging when we're watching our kids play sports. The way we drive our vehicle will not be angry and aggressive. We will not pursue a toxic masculinity that will advance us by the world's standards, but we will do whatever we can to pursue a Christ-like identity that values humility, grace, and kindness to others. Our actions will reflect the light of God.

Jesus' claim to be the light of the world extended the light of God to us. And since there is no darkness in Him, when He lives in our hearts, every aspect of our lives should be a light to others.

QUESTIONS

1. This may be a tough devotional. It causes us to look at our actions and recognize that we've made mistakes. What are some ways your actions have not aligned with the character of God?

2. When we recognize the mistakes we've made, the key is to not make them again. How can you guard yourself from making those same mistakes again?

3. Pray that God would change your heart and help you to walk in His light.

DAY 12
THE LIGHT OF THE WORLD

You are the light of the world. A city set on a hill cannot be hidden. Nor do people light a lamp and put it under a basket, but on a stand, and it gives light to all in the house. In the same way, let your light shine before others, so that they may see your good works and give glory to your Father who is in heaven. - Matthew 5:14-16

At first glance, this passage might seem contradictory to the theme of this chapter. Aren't we talking about the "I am" statements of Jesus and not the "you are" statements? Yes. And this is very good news.

These verses are part of a larger passage of Scripture called "The Sermon on the Mount" found in Matthew 5-7. This sermon begins with a section called The Beatitudes and then moves to more topical and moral lessons. In Matthew 5:13-16, Jesus began talking about His disciples, the ones whom He was teaching. He calls His followers "the light of the world." What an incredible way to describe a group of tax collectors, fishermen, and outcasts! How could they possibly be the light of the world? What light had they ever brought to this world on their own?

That's the beauty of it all. Jesus makes them, and us, the light of the world. We don't shine with our own light; we reflect His. Jesus called His followers the light of the world in the same way He called Himself the light of the world. By saying His followers and Himself are both lights He was not claiming equality between Himself and His followers. It was more of an invitation for His followers to join Him in ministry.

I love the part of this verse when Jesus says God will be praised when others see His follower's good deeds. It's not the doer of the deeds that is praised, but the source of the goodness that prompted the deeds that is praised. Just like the moon, while not producing any light of its own, illuminates the world at night by reflecting the sun, so it is with Jesus' followers reflecting the light of God to the world.

When Jesus lives in us, we take part in His ministry to the world and shine our light (which is His light) into the dark places. In Jesus' prayer for all believers on the night before He was crucified found in John 17:22-23, He prayed, "The glory that you have given me I have given to them, that they may be one even as we are one, I in them and you in me, that they may become perfectly one, so that the world may know that you sent me and loved them even as you loved me." Jesus is the light of the world because He and God are one. Followers of Jesus are also the light of the world because He has given us His glory. And the world can know God by this incredible privilege believers have as we take part in His ministry to the world.

The only way a group of outcast men could be considered the light of the world is for them to reflect a greater light that is within them—the light of Jesus.

QUESTIONS

1. How would you rate yourself as the light of the world? Do you think you do a good job of showing the light of Jesus to the world through your deeds?

2. What ways can you point people to God if you receive praise for something you've done?

3. What ways can you reflect the light of Jesus today? Is there something you can do for someone in need? Is there a neighbor you can help? Is there a coworker you can encourage? Think of a way to be the light of the world by your actions today, then do it.

DAY 13
THE LIGHT OF THE WORLD

And you are my sheep, human sheep of my pasture, and I am your God, declares the Lord GOD. - Ezekiel 34:31

Before we start today's devotional, read Ezekiel 34 in its entirety. The main verse will make much more sense when you read the whole chapter. This is such a powerful chapter when we realize what was happening during this time. Israel was in captivity in Babylon because of their centuries-long disobedience to God. Ezekiel was a priest who wrote this book during the Babylonian exile. When we read Ezekiel's words to the Israelites, we see several things happening. First, this was a warning to the leaders of Israel because of their poor leadership. Secondly, it prophesied that God would deliver them from exile. He said, "He Himself" will be their shepherd and gather the sheep that have been scattered. Next, it was a warning to the people of Israel that God would judge their actions. And finally, it was a proclamation that God would place one shepherd over Israel: a leader from the lineage of His servant, David.

Ezekiel is not claiming that David would be the king again. David lived some 400 years before Ezekiel wrote these words. He is saying that the good shepherd would come from the line of David and would be an even better and more perfect version of the greatest king in Israel's history. To this book's original hearers and readers, two promises were being made about the good shepherd that was to come. God said, "I myself" several times when referring to the shepherd that would lead them. This is a divine shepherd. Then He said that David would lead them. This is an earthly shepherd. There's only one person who could be both.

As we look at Jesus' "I am" statements in John 10, this passage comes to life. Jesus is both fully divine and fully human! When He claimed He was the good shepherd, the Pharisees listening to Him probably got angry because they were leading their people, the sheep, poorly, and Jesus was calling them out.

Throughout the New Testament, we see Jesus becoming the answer for all the shortcomings of Israel. My favorite Old Testament professor at Beeson Divinity School, where I attended seminary, was Dr. Mark Gignilliat. He once said, "Jesus is for Israel what she couldn't be for herself." This is never truer than Jesus' ability to be the good shepherd. He is the only one who could undo what they did to themselves. He is the only one worthy of being called "the good shepherd."

If Jesus can undo all the damage a nation caused herself and the pain and strife that came with their disobedience for centuries, just think about what He can do for you. There is nothing you have brought upon yourself that Jesus can't fix. Sure, there will be consequences, just like there were for Israel, but Jesus offers hope, grace, and love that will guide you to a place where you will be cared for and where you can be restored.

QUESTIONS

1. Take some time to study this chapter. Write down some of the ways the bad shepherds of Israel led their people.

2. Now, write down what God promises He will do instead.

3. What have you done to yourself, your family, or your friends that you must hand over to God so that He can undo it?

4. Pray that Jesus will give you the strength to hand it over to Him and let Him restore whatever it is.

DAY 14
THE DOOR & THE GOOD SHEPHERD

So Jesus again said to them, "Truly, truly, I say to you, I am the door of the sheep."
- John 10:7

I am the good shepherd. The good shepherd lays down his life for the sheep.
- John 10:11

This chapter will be a little different than the previous two as we have combined two "I am" statements into one week: "I am the door of the sheep" and "I am the good shepherd." Both images are that of the same person: a shepherd. As we will see, Jesus embodies this image of the good shepherd through the different roles He describes.

This image of the shepherd is prevalent throughout the Bible. It is an old profession, and we see it referenced in the Old and New Testaments. It's safe to say that most of us reading this devotional are not shepherds. However, there are traits we will see this week that make sense when we picture Jesus as the good shepherd.

If we look at John 10, we see aspects of Jesus' character in how He describes the actions of a good shepherd. As you read this passage, begin to think about ways in which Jesus exemplifies these traits. Below are a few examples found in this passage.

The sheep listen to Jesus' voice. He is worthy of respect and authority.
Jesus calls His sheep by name. He knows His sheep on a personal level.
Jesus leads and leads in a way that keeps the sheep safe with their needs met.
Jesus goes ahead of all His sheep. He leads from the front to find green pastures.
Jesus' sheep recognize His voice. The words He says are life-giving and good.
Jesus cares for His sheep. He does not run from danger but cares deeply for His flock.
Jesus lays down His life for His sheep. He did what was best for His sheep, even when it meant dying.

Not knowing the whole story, it's easy to see why the Pharisees were divided and why some thought Jesus was crazy. However, we know the whole story. We know Jesus truly is the good shepherd.

Spend some time preparing your heart to see Jesus as the good shepherd this week. There are many more ways than those listed above that you may think of as we spend time in God's Word this week. Read the words to the 1836 hymn, Savior, Like a Shepherd Lead Us, written by Dorothy A. Thrupp, as a prayer to begin this week as we study the "I am" statements found in John 10.

SAVIOR, LIKE A SHEPHERD LEAD US,
MUCH WE NEED THY TENDER CARE;
IN THY PLEASANT PASTURES FEED US,
FOR OUR USE THY FOLDS PREPARE:
WE ARE THINE, DO THOU BEFRIEND US,
BE THE GUARDIAN OF OUR WAY;
KEEP THY FLOCK, FROM SIN DEFEND US,
SEEK US WHEN WE GO ASTRAY:
THOU HAST PROMISED TO RECEIVE US,
POOR AND SINFUL THOUGH WE BE;
THOU HAST MERCY TO RELIEVE US,
GRACE TO CLEANSE, AND POW'R TO FREE:
EARLY LET US SEEK THY FAVOR,
EARLY LET US DO THY WILL;
BLESSED LORD AND ONLY SAVIOR,
WITH THY LOVE OUR BOSOMS FILL:
BLESSED JESUS, BLESSED JESUS,
THOU HAST LOVED US, LOVE US STILL.

DAY 15
THE DOOR & THE GOOD SHEPHERD

The LORD is my shepherd; I shall not want. He makes me lie down in green pastures. He leads me beside still waters. He restores my soul. He leads me in paths of righteousness for his name's sake. Even though I walk through the valley of the shadow of death, I will fear no evil, for you are with me; your rod and your staff, they comfort me. - Psalm 23:1-4

When I want to experience God in His creation, I go to the water. Whether fly fishing, hiking, camping, or simply listening to the gentle ripples of a stream, I'm drawn to the water. Or, as Norman Maclean wrote in his 1976 book, A River Runs Through It, "I am haunted by waters." Being near the water restores my soul, and cares seem to fade away along with the passing current. There's a reason the African-American spiritual says, "I've got peace like a river."

When David, the writer of Psalm 23, refers to God as his shepherd, he understands the peace that only God can bring. Let's dissect this passage a little by asking questions of the text.

When would you lie down in green pastures? Sheep would only lie down where the grass is green if they are completely content and satisfied. If they are lying down, they feel safe, and they don't have any needs. Just as David said, "I shall not want," God as shepherd provides for all our needs.

Why is it important that the waters are still? Still waters indicate no danger of being harmed by the rushing currents, where the sheep could get swept away or where the sound would disguise any approaching enemy. Again, the sheep are safe from harm and have access to the water they need because of the shepherd who cares for their needs.

Why would someone walk through the deep, dark valley on purpose? Just like in the wilderness that David knew well, where the long shadows of the land could hide unavoidable dangers, sometimes it's impossible to avoid the darkest times in your life. Whether it is a season of pain and suffering, depression, doubt, guilt, or fear, dark times come into our lives uninvited. Relying on God during those times is vital. God's presence reassured David during those dark times.

Why would a rod and staff offer comfort to the psalmist? The rod and staff were used for protection against outside enemies and wild beasts. David was familiar with the damage the rod could do to dangerous lions and bears—he'd experienced it firsthand. But these tools were also used for correction. The shepherd would use the rod and staff to correct the sheep and lead them on the right path and away from danger. We should find comfort in God's protection and correction because He cares for us.

When Jesus claimed He was the good shepherd, He embodied this divine shepherd to whom David was writing. Thousands of years after these words were written, Jesus still fulfills these Scriptures by protecting and leading us as the ultimate good shepherd.

QUESTIONS

1. Where is your green pasture? In what ways does God fulfill your needs?

2. Recall a time when God protected you from a dangerous situation like the valley of the shadow of death. What did you learn about God in this season of life?

3. In what ways can you find comfort in God's correction?

DAY 16
THE DOOR & THE GOOD SHEPHERD

I am the door. If anyone enters by me, he will be saved and will go in and out and find pasture. The thief comes only to steal and kill and destroy. I came that they may have life and have it abundantly. - John 10:9-10

It's a common trope used in movies. A group of villains is approaching a weaker character, and a hero steps in and says, "If you're going to get to him, you've got to go through me." Although it's cheesy and probably overused, I love scenes like that. There's no hope for the helpless character, especially against the gang of bullies who are bigger, stronger, and outnumber him. But then hope shows up (most of the time, either on a motorcycle or wearing a letterman's jacket), and all of a sudden, the weaker character has a chance, not because of some newly found strength, but because of the strength of the hero.

Read John 10:1-10 before going any further.

When Jesus refers to Himself as "the door of the sheep," He is referring to the practice of the shepherd positioning his body in the doorway of the sheep pen. In those days, shepherds would sleep in the doorway and guard the sheep at night. Nothing would come through the gateway to steal or attack the sheep because the good shepherd would be there to stop it. Jesus is the hero who places Himself between the weak sheep and the dangers of the enemy.

Just as we saw in Ezekiel 34, "thieves and robbers" could refer to the bad leaders of Israel who, like bad shepherds, led the sheep astray and only looked after their own needs. Thieves and robbers could also refer to false prophets and people who had claimed to be the Messiah. Either way, Jesus claims that of all the people who have come before, and all that would come after, He is the only way for His sheep to be led to salvation.

Jesus juxtaposes Himself with the thieves and robbers by stating what each of them offers. The thief only comes to steal, kill, and destroy. But Jesus offers life! And not just any life, a full life! The kind of life that David writes about in Psalm 23. It's the kind of life where we are never in want, and God, the good shepherd, supplies our every need. The salvation that Jesus offers is the promise of eternal salvation and a here-and-now salvation—the good life!

QUESTIONS

1. The sheep in this passage only listen to the good shepherd because they can distinguish His voice. Would you say that describes you? Or does the voice of the good shepherd, Jesus, get lost in the noise of the thieves and robbers?

2. How can you train your heart to better recognize the voice of the good shepherd?

3. What are ways the thief is trying to steal, kill, and destroy the good life that God has for you?

4. Pray that God would intervene and fight the thieves and robbers in your life who are trying to deny you the fullest life that trusting Jesus brings.

DAY 17
THE DOOR & THE GOOD SHEPHERD

Enter by the narrow gate. For the gate is wide and the way is easy that leads to destruction, and those who enter by it are many. For the gate is narrow and the way is hard that leads to life, and those who find it are few. - Matthew 7:13-14

This passage is found at the end of the Sermon on the Mount. It is the first of four "either/or" type statements: narrow or wide gates, true or false prophets, true or false disciples, and wise or foolish builders. These final four lessons in Jesus' sermon are hard ones. They divide people into two groups. Either you are for Jesus, or you are against Him. There is no middle ground.

Let's look at the two gates that Jesus describes. The wide gate is at the end of a broad road. This destination is one of destruction, and the saddest part is that many people will enter through it. This road is paved with philosophies such as "get all you can because you only live once," "I'm going to get mine," "do whatever feels right," "live your best life," "that's my truth," and "I deserve…." These types of thinking are prevalent in our world today. The wide road is self-serving and self-centered. Just look at the culture we're living in; very few people care about anyone but themselves. This is a wide road, and it is full of godless philosophies that are leading to destruction.

The second gate is small, and a narrow road leads to this gate. And sadly, only a few will find it. This road is paved with truth, humility, selflessness, love for others, and the fruit of the spirit. It is completely counter-cultural to be on the narrow road. If you don't believe me, be kind, patient, and loving to the next restaurant worker you meet. Watch how they respond to the love of Christ shown through your actions. They might look at you like you're from another planet. And while people resist traveling this road, they desperately want what it offers. They want to be loved and accepted just as they are, but they shun the one standing at the gate, saying, "Come to me, all who labor and are heavy laden, and I will give you rest" (Matt. 11:28).

There is only one way to the Father: through Jesus Christ, the door. The road that leads to Jesus is narrow because He has a standard, which is there to protect His children, not to keep them from having a good life or to suppress their joy. Jesus offers joy through freedom and, as we read yesterday in John 10, a full life for all who follow Him.

QUESTIONS

1. How can you be a light for those on the broad road headed toward the wide gate of destruction?

2. How can you show Christ's love to others through your actions?

3. Pray that God would give you strength to stay focused on Him as you trek the narrow way.

DAY 18
THE DOOR & THE GOOD SHEPHERD

They shall hunger no more, neither thirst anymore; the sun shall not strike them, nor any scorching heat. For the Lamb in the midst of the throne will be their shepherd, and he will guide them to springs of living water, and God will wipe away every tear from their eyes.
- Revelation 7:16-17

As we conclude this week's study of Jesus' "I am" statements about the "good shepherd," one recurring theme that we need to remember is the constant looking forward and backward that happens simultaneously. Ezekiel, David, and others were looking forward to the coming good shepherd centuries before Jesus was born. And then, when Jesus arrived, the writers of the New Testament constantly looked back to the Old Testament prophecies to show that Jesus was who He said He was. Even though He fulfilled the promises of the good shepherd that was to come, people still didn't accept Him.

Then, in John's Revelation, after Jesus' resurrection, we see a future vision of the good shepherd. This passage in Revelation shows us that in the end times, Jesus, the Lamb of God, seated on the throne of heaven, is the shepherd who still cares for His people. Just like in Psalm 23, Jesus, the good shepherd, will lead the slain by springs of living water. This verse is not only a reference to Psalm 23, but it is also a direct reference to Isaiah 49:10: "They shall not hunger or thirst, neither scorching wind nor sun shall strike them, for he who has pity on them will lead them, and by springs of water will guide them."

When we think about Jesus, the good shepherd, we see that He was, is, and will be our guide for all eternity. We can have the assurance that He can be trusted. We can trust Him with our life here and now and with our souls forever. And we, as the sheep of His flock, only need to rest in His leadership.

As we learn more about the good shepherd, we can also learn about His sheep. While no man wants to be considered a sheep, perhaps we should humble ourselves and embrace this role as sheep in the flock of the shepherd king. His sheep are cared for, they are content, their needs are met, they are protected, and they find rest in the presence of their shepherd. Do you see the theme here? The sheep aren't trying to earn their shepherd's love and aren't working to gain favor in the shepherd's eyes. They are loved by the shepherd simply because they are His sheep. They are valuable because He says they are valuable. The sheep are powerless without the shepherd. They know Him, trust Him, and follow Him because He is worthy to be followed. I would rather be a sheep in God's pasture than a wolf in the devil's pack.

QUESTIONS

1. In what ways has the good shepherd shown Himself to be trustworthy in your life?

2. What the good shepherd offers His sheep is far better than what the sheep can attain on their own. How can you be a better sheep?

3. What areas of your life do you need to surrender to God as your good shepherd?

DAY 19
THE RESURRECTION AND THE LIFE

Jesus said to her, "I am the resurrection and the life. Whoever believes in me, though he die, yet shall he live, and everyone who lives and believes in me shall never die. Do you believe this?" - John 11:25-26

Over the next several days, we will examine what Jesus meant when He said, "I am the resurrection and the life." In this passage, Mary and Martha's brother, Lazarus, had become sick and died. While Jesus could've kept him from dying, He chose not to so that God would get the glory through his death. Jesus decided not to keep Lazarus from dying so that people could understand what it meant to be resurrected. When Martha came to Jesus and said He could have kept him from dying, Jesus told her Lazarus would rise again. She thought He was talking about the resurrection of the dead in the last days, but Jesus said to her, "I am the resurrection." Jesus said that Lazarus wouldn't have to wait until the last days to be raised from the grave because God was about to do something amazing.

The interesting thing here is that Lazarus was dead, and Jesus resurrected him. It's easy to compare this to Jesus' resurrection. But the obvious difference here is that when Jesus died and rose again, He never experienced death again. Lazarus would one day die again. It's almost as if Lazarus was only resuscitated rather than resurrected. The only person to be resurrected once and for all was Jesus. Jesus died, rose again, and never died again. Lazarus died, rose from the grave, died again, and will be resurrected in the last days.

What we must remember about Jesus' death, burial, and resurrection is the purpose for each. Jesus' death on the cross purchased forgiveness of sin for all who would believe. His resurrection from the grave gave eternal life to all who would believe. Jesus had to show that a resurrection was possible because they'd never seen it before. He was setting the example once again for what was to come.

Think about how far we've come from the Wright brothers and their rudimentary airplane. Because they showed the world what was possible, that man could fly, we have been to outer space. So many times, we don't know what is possible because we've not been shown an example.

When Jesus performed this miracle of raising Lazarus from the grave, He proved that resurrection was possible and could only be done through believing in Him. Think about the other things in your life that seem impossible but are possible through Jesus. Is your relationship with someone in your family broken? Is there someone in your life who seems impossible to love? Is your relationship with your parents seemingly unfixable? Is the weight of this world feeling too heavy to bear? All of these things seem impossible to overcome, but through Jesus, they can be.

Read Psalm 30:1-10 as your prayer for today.

[1] I WILL EXTOL YOU, O LORD, FOR YOU HAVE DRAWN ME UP
AND HAVE NOT LET MY FOES REJOICE OVER ME.
[2] O LORD MY GOD, I CRIED TO YOU FOR HELP,
AND YOU HAVE HEALED ME.
[3] O LORD, YOU HAVE BROUGHT UP MY SOUL FROM SHEOL;
YOU RESTORED ME TO LIFE FROM AMONG THOSE WHO GO DOWN TO THE PIT.

[4] SING PRAISES TO THE LORD, O YOU HIS SAINTS,
AND GIVE THANKS TO HIS HOLY NAME.
[5] FOR HIS ANGER IS BUT FOR A MOMENT,
AND HIS FAVOR IS FOR A LIFETIME.
WEEPING MAY TARRY FOR THE NIGHT,
BUT JOY COMES WITH THE MORNING.

[6] AS FOR ME, I SAID IN MY PROSPERITY,
"I SHALL NEVER BE MOVED."
[7] BY YOUR FAVOR, O LORD,
YOU MADE MY MOUNTAIN STAND STRONG;
YOU HID YOUR FACE;
I WAS DISMAYED.

[8] TO YOU, O LORD, I CRY,
AND TO THE LORD I PLEAD FOR MERCY:
[9] "WHAT PROFIT IS THERE IN MY DEATH,
IF I GO DOWN TO THE PIT?
WILL THE DUST PRAISE YOU?
WILL IT TELL OF YOUR FAITHFULNESS?
[10] HEAR, O LORD, AND BE MERCIFUL TO ME!
O LORD, BE MY HELPER!"

DAY 20
THE RESURRECTION AND THE LIFE

Then he said to me, "Prophesy over these bones, and say to them, O dry bones, hear the word of the LORD. Thus says the Lord GOD to these bones: Behold, I will cause breath to enter you, and you shall live. And I will lay sinews upon you, and will cause flesh to come upon you, and cover you with skin, and put breath in you, and you shall live, and you shall know that I am the LORD." - Ezekiel 37:4-6

Before we jump into today's devotional, read Ezekiel 37:1-14. Full transparency here: this is a wild passage. There are a lot of strange things going on here. But this passage gives us a great example of what it means to have life through Christ.

The Hebrew word ruwach (roo-akh) is repeated in this passage. It is the word for wind, breath, and spirit. Ruwach is the word used throughout the Old Testament to refer to the Spirit of the Lord, the Holy Spirit. Remember that as we unpack this wild story.

In this passage, Ezekiel is led by the Spirit of God to a valley filled with dry bones. As he is surveying this grim scene of this mass grave, the Spirit asks, "Can these bones live?" What a question! These bones are dry and lifeless. These bones can't come back to life; they are dead. That is true, aside from God. But with God's Spirit inside them, they came to life.

The bones and the tendons, muscles, and flesh were there. But it wasn't until the breath, the Spirit, entered these bodies that they came to life. Just like in Genesis 2, when God breathed life into Adam, He breathed His Spirit into these dry bones, and they came to life. God showed what He was about to do to Israel, who had become dead and dry like this pile of bones. Although they began to look alive on the outside, they weren't truly living until the Spirit of God was with them.

All of us are like this pile of bones. While we might look alive on the outside, we are lifeless without the Spirit of God. You are not truly alive until the Holy Spirit is living inside you. We can only receive the Holy Spirit through belief in Jesus Christ, the resurrection, and the life. When Jesus said, "I am the resurrection," not only was He showing what He could do for Lazarus, but He was showing what must happen for each of us as well.

QUESTIONS

1. What areas of your life are "lifeless"? Where do you feel dry right now?

2. Have you surrendered these areas of your life to God and asked the Spirit to breathe life into them? If not, why not? If so, what has been the response?

3. Spend time in prayer and reflection today, asking God to reveal places in your life that need a fresh "breath" from the Holy Spirit to invigorate and revitalize them. Listen to what God is telling you. Humble yourself and be open to the changes He desires to make.

DAY 21
THE RESURRECTION AND THE LIFE

But the angel said to the women, "Do not be afraid, for I know that you seek Jesus who was crucified. He is not here, for he has risen, as he said. Come, see the place where he lay. Then go quickly and tell his disciples that he has risen from the dead, and behold, he is going before you to Galilee; there you will see him. See, I have told you." - Matthew 28:5-7

What comes to mind when you think about industry leaders or companies who have set the standard in their field? Nike? Disney? Netflix? Tesla? Apple? Google? Amazon? These companies might not have been the first in their field, but they raised the standard for everyone who follows them. Think about what these companies have accomplished. They have raised the expectations for efficiency, expanded our technology, and redefined the customer experience. They have changed our thinking about the future by showing the world what was possible.

Can you imagine the hope that was lost when they buried Jesus? Everything, and I mean everything He had taught them, was hanging on what would happen next. If He stayed dead, nothing mattered. The miracles were pointless, His death was in vain, and the hope of forgiveness of sins and eternal life was lost. But then imagine the hope regained when they heard that He had risen and saw the empty tomb where His body once lay.

When Mary and Mary Magdalene arrived at the tomb where Jesus was buried, they were shocked at the events that unfolded before them. There was an earthquake, an angel appeared, the stone covering Jesus' tomb was rolled back, and Jesus was gone. Matthew 28:8 says, "So they departed quickly from the tomb with fear and great joy, and ran to tell his disciples." Everything that Jesus said had come true! Jesus had prophesied His resurrection, and they had witnessed Jesus raise Lazarus from the dead. Even though they didn't completely understand, it was beginning to make sense to them.

Jesus—the resurrection and the life—is the standard of what those who follow Him in faith will experience in the final resurrection. The world didn't even know eternal life was possible before Jesus set the standard. While we don't fully understand it, we trust Jesus with our souls for eternity because He conquered death and rose from the grave. He changed our thoughts about our future by showing us what was possible.

QUESTIONS

1. When you evaluate your life rhythms, in what ways are you living for eternity?

2. How is your life different knowing Jesus rose from the grave to give you eternal life?

3. What would you change about your habits and routines if you truly believed you were an eternal being who will live forever?

DAY 22
THE RESURRECTION AND THE LIFE

Jesus answered them, "Destroy this temple, and in three days I will raise it up." - John 2:19

In John 2:13-22, Jesus had finally tired of the hypocrisy of the church leaders and was disgusted with how people were regarding sacrifice in the Temple. Not only were these people selling animals inside the Temple, but many believe they had increased the price of the animals to make a profit off travelers who were in town for the upcoming Passover feast. When Jesus saw that the Temple had become a place where people were exploiting others in the name of God, He got angry and cleared it by force.

I always liked this passage in John because it showed Jesus' human nature when He got angry. The anger Jesus felt was righteous anger, a holy anger that was not sinful like our anger often is. This righteous anger was in response to evil people exploiting the poor and doing so in the name of His Father, God. We should all have a wave of righteous anger when people are treated unjustly.

The next part of this passage shows Jesus' divine nature. After Jesus cleared the Temple and claimed it was His father's house, the Jews questioned His authority to do these things. Jesus challenged them to "Destroy this temple, and I will raise it again in three days." This confused the Jews because they thought He was talking about the actual Temple. But, in reality, He was talking about His own body. This didn't make sense to anyone until after Jesus' resurrection.

What do we know about the Temple? People came to make sacrifices for their sins to be forgiven, worship God, and find rest and comfort. For Jesus to indirectly refer to Himself as the temple, He foreshadowed that He would be the atoning sacrifice for our sins, give us rest, and rise from the grave in three days.

And after Jesus was murdered on the cross, buried, and rose from the grave, all of these came true. And because of Jesus' resurrection and the gift of the Holy Spirit, our bodies are now the temples where the Holy Spirit resides. In 1 Corinthians 6:19-20, Paul says, "Or do you not know that your body is a temple of the Holy Spirit within you, whom you have from God? You are not your own, for you were bought with a price. So glorify God in your body." Now, because of Jesus, the resurrection and the life, the Holy Spirit abides in the hearts of all who believe. So, how, then, should we live?

QUESTIONS

1. How should your life be different since the Holy Spirit lives in your heart?

2. How should you view sin, knowing that what grieves and angers God should be what grieves and angers you?

3. Pray that God would give you the strength and wisdom to act in a way that reflects the Holy Spirit within you.

DAY 23
THE RESURRECTION AND THE LIFE

When I saw him, I fell at his feet as though dead. But he laid his right hand on me, saying, "Fear not, I am the first and the last, and the living one. I died, and behold I am alive forevermore, and I have the keys of Death and Hades."
- Revelation 1:17-18

Revelation can be confusing at times. Scholars have interpreted it in many different ways throughout history. Volumes of books have been written, both scholarly and fictional, attempting to interpret it. However, one thing is certain: the book's purpose is to exalt Jesus as the only one worthy to die for the forgiveness of sins.

Jesus Himself revealed these things to John so that he could share them. In the beginning of the book of Revelation, Jesus is described as "firstborn from the dead," meaning that He is the one who defeated death through the resurrection. Because of the resurrection, Jesus gave us freedom and a full life. But the word "freedom" is sometimes misunderstood.

The freedom we have from Jesus' resurrection is not a freedom TO sin, but a freedom FROM sin. Paul wrote in Romans 6:5-7, "For if we have been united with him in a death like his, we shall certainly be united with him in a resurrection like his. We know that our old self was crucified with him in order that the body of sin might be brought to nothing, so that we would no longer be enslaved to sin. For one who has died has been set free from sin." It is our sinful nature to sin. We don't need freedom to sin—that comes naturally. What we need is freedom from the bondage that sin has on our lives. Without the resurrection, we are helpless in our ability to overcome sin. But with the resurrection of Jesus, we have the ability, through the blood of Jesus, to live a life where we are not ruled by sin.

Jesus' resurrection does not give you the right or freedom to do as you please and live however you think is best. This freedom means that now we are allowed to return to fellowship with God through His son, Jesus, and live a life that is pleasing to Him. Why do we continue to treat our salvation as a license to sin? You're missing the point if you see salvation as permission to sin because you are covered by grace. This is what Dietrich Bonhoeffer calls "cheap grace." In The Cost of Discipleship, Bonhoeffer wrote, "Cheap grace is grace without discipleship, grace without the cross, grace without Jesus Christ, living and incarnate."

Will you slip up on occasion? Of course, but know that the true freedom of salvation does not move you toward sin; it gives you the freedom to move away from sin and grow closer to God—a freedom we didn't have after sin entered the world until Jesus.

QUESTIONS

1. What needs to happen in your life for you to recognize the power of Jesus' resurrection was to free you from sin and not to sin?

2. How are you fighting against "cheap grace?" Are you in a discipleship group? Studying God's word regularly? Serving others?

3. Identify an area in your life where you are still moving toward sin rather than toward God.

DAY 24
THE WAY, THE TRUTH, AND THE LIFE

Jesus said to him, "I am the way, and the truth, and the life. No one comes to the Father except through me." - John 14:6

Over the next few days, we will examine what this "I am" statement means and how we will apply it to our lives. This is one of the more familiar of the seven statements we cover in this book. Jesus saying, "I am the way, and the truth, and the life" was a proclamation of His deity and His way of offering comfort to His disciples.

In this passage in John 14, Jesus told His disciples about a place He would go to prepare for them in heaven. Thomas said, "Lord, we don't know where you are going, so how can we know the way?" Then, Jesus says this incredible line, "I am the way, and the truth, and the life."

Jesus didn't say "a way, a truth, or a life." When the question was asked, "How can we know the way," Jesus said, "I am the way." Not only is He the way, but He is also "the truth," reassuring Thomas and others that they can believe Him. And He is "the life," reassuring them that they too will have eternal life. He cannot be separated from the three components of this "I am" statement. Believing in Jesus means that you believe He is who He said He is.

Don't get me wrong; believing Jesus is all of these can be difficult for some. These claims are so bold that there's no wiggle room for who Jesus is. C.S. Lewis talks about this in Mere Christianity. He logically argues that someone who claims to be the Son of God is either a liar, lunatic, or Lord. We know that Jesus was not a liar nor a lunatic, so the logical conclusion is that Jesus truly is the Son of God and Lord of all.

This "I am" statement addresses the disciples' fears. Jesus' words were intended to comfort them. He reassured them that they could follow Him because He is the way, believe Him because He is the truth, and live for Him because He is the life. Unpacking each of these claims is important, but it's also important that they were coupled together. They are not the same claims, but they are all interrelated and embodied by Jesus, the Son of God.

Just as the disciples struggled to understand all Jesus meant when He said who He was and failed time after time to comprehend all that He was talking about, some of us need help believing the hard things. Trusting that Jesus is the way, the truth, and the life is hard. As we begin studying this "I am" statement over the next few days, let the words of the father of the mute child in Mark 9:23-24 be your prayer: "And Jesus said to him, 'If you can'! All things are possible for one who believes.' Immediately the father of the child cried out and said, 'I believe; help my unbelief!'"

As we begin studying this "I am" statement over the next few days, let the words of this hymn be your prayer. This song, Be Thou My Vision, was written by Dallán Forgaill in the 6th century and is considered to be one of the oldest hymns ever written.

BE THOU MY VISION, O LORD OF MY HEART;

NAUGHT BE ALL ELSE TO ME, SAVE THAT THOU ART -

THOU MY BEST THOUGHT, BY DAY OR BY NIGHT;

WAKING OR SLEEPING, THY PRESENCE MY LIGHT.

BE THOU MY WISDOM, AND THOU MY TRUE WORD;

I EVER WITH THEE AND THOU WITH ME, LORD.

THOU MY GREAT FATHER; THINE OWN MAY I BE,

THOU IN ME DWELLING AND I ONE WITH THEE.

DAY 25
THE WAY, THE TRUTH, AND THE LIFE

And there is salvation in no one else, for there is no other name under heaven given among men by which we must be saved. - Acts 4:12

The name of God was so powerful to early Jews that they wouldn't say it when reading Scriptures in the synagogue. Pronouncing God's name, Yahweh, or YHWH, as it was written in Hebrew, was considered sinful, and they would say the word "Adonai" instead of the correct pronunciation of Yahweh or Jehovah. Early transcribers who would copy Scriptures would undergo cleansing before and after they wrote the letters for YHWH. We must understand that God's name was that important and treated with reverence as we look at the following passages.

Before we look at Acts 4, read Isaiah 45:22-25. If you notice the two instances where LORD is used, the original Hebrew is YHWH or the name of God. One instance is, "'To me every knee shall bow, every tongue shall swear allegiance.' Only in the LORD, it shall be said of me,are righteousness and strength." Does this passage sound familiar?

Now, read Philippians 2:9-11. Notice anything? Paul wrote, "Therefore God has highly exalted him and bestowed on him the name that is above every name, so that at the name of Jesus every knee should bow, in heaven and on earth and under the earth, and every tongue confess that Jesus Christ is Lord, to the glory of God the Father." This was no mistake. Paul was showing the church in Philippi that Jesus was, in fact, YHWH.

When we see Peter proclaim the same to Annas, the high priest, and his family, they would've known that Peter also claimed that Jesus was YHWH from Isaiah.

When we look at other ways that God saved humanity from the Old Testament, they all fell short of eternal salvation. God preserved Noah and his family from the flood with an ark. He provided a ram for Abraham to sacrifice instead of his son. God saved the Israelites from death with the lamb's blood over the doorposts in Egypt. God delivered the Israelites through the desert with Moses. Everything points to Jesus from the Bible's beginning to the end. When Jesus proclaimed, "I am the way," He was staking His claim as the only way to God. There was no other way before Him, and there would be no other way after Him. Jesus is the way, and there is no other name by which we must be saved.

QUESTIONS

1. Spend time praying today to thank God for His son, Jesus.

2. Pray that you will never underestimate the power of Jesus' name.

3. Pray that you would not be distracted by the lies of this world that claim there are multiple ways to God, the Father.

DAY 26
THE WAY, THE TRUTH, AND THE LIFE

The sum of your word is truth, and every one of your righteous rules endures forever. - Psalm 119:160

Truth has come under attack over the last few years. Terms like "relative truth," "alternative facts," and phrases like "that's my truth" have permeated our culture so much that claiming a solid truth in anything is more complicated. Telling the truth is sometimes more dangerous than telling a lie.

We live in an upside-down world where truth is punished and lying is rewarded. Several years ago, I was pulled over by the police for having a missing headlight. The officer approached my window and asked if I knew I had a blown headlight. I told him I did, but I had not yet had a chance to fix it. He shook his head and said, "You should've said no. Now I have to give you a ticket." Knowing the law and telling the truth about my breaking the law had a more severe punishment than lying about the situation.

When Jesus states that He is the truth, He is stating that His words are true, His ways are true, and He will do what He said He will do. Just as the Psalmist wrote, "The sum of your word is truth, and every one of your righteous rules endures forever," Jesus embodied the words of God and fulfilled God's law.

Because we know the law, we know that sin is in our lives. The truth is sin separates God and humankind. There is only one way for our sins to be atoned for: through sacrifice. The only true sacrifice that can cover our sins for eternity is Jesus. There are not enough good works we can do to earn salvation. No alternate religion will allow us to reach enlightenment and become like God. No individual truth will set you free in a different way than someone else. The truth is that there is one way, and His name is Jesus.

When I was given a ticket for not having a headlight, I had to pay the price for breaking the law. Because each of us has broken God's laws and is sinful by nature, we, too, must pay the price. However, because Jesus died on the cross for our sins, His blood has forgiven our transgressions and paid in full. That's the truth.

QUESTIONS

1. Take some time today to get real about your sins. Dig deep and pray that God will reveal your sins to you. Sins you've committed, the good things you failed to do, the times when you should've helped the helpless, and the sins you buried deep in your past.

2. There is no sin that is too great where the truth of God's forgiveness cannot be reached. Pray that God would heal your heart, your past, and your relationships with His truth.

DAY 27
THE WAY, THE TRUTH, AND THE LIFE

In the beginning was the Word, and the Word was with God, and the Word was God. He was in the beginning with God. All things were made through him, and without him was not any thing made that was made. In him was life, and the life was the light of men. The light shines in the darkness, and the darkness has not overcome it. - John 1:1-5

When John talks about the Word being with God in the beginning, he is talking about Jesus. Jesus is the Word incarnate. That means that Jesus was the Word that became flesh. Jesus didn't come into existence when He was born in Bethlehem; He has always existed but humbled Himself to become human to save us from our sins and give us life.

In the beloved children's book by C.S. Lewis, The Lion, the Witch, and the Wardrobe, the White Witch had cursed Narnia. It was cold and covered with snow, void of life, and those living in the land were oppressed under her rule. Anyone who opposed the White Witch would be imprisoned and turned to stone. In a grim scene near the end of the book, Aslan, Susan, and Lucy are walking through a courtyard of stone statues. Each of these statues was once a living being, but they had been frozen by the White Witch and turned into lifeless stone structures. The scene became even more heartbreaking when Lucy recognized Mr. Tumnus, her friend from earlier in the book. They thought there was no hope for their friend, but a beautiful thing happened. Aslan, the Jesus figure in the book, began to breathe his breath on each of the statues. Suddenly, these lifeless creatures began to move and come back to life.

Just like these statues, we can become cold and hardened like stone because of Satan's influence over this world. But Jesus, the life-giver, can break through our hardened hearts and give us new life. A heart of stone is a dangerous thing. It can keep us from seeing people who are hurting. It can make us racially biased. It can make us say unkind words. It can blind us from our shortcomings and make us more attuned to the sins of others. But Jesus is the life. He loves us, forgives us, and helps us have a full life here and for eternity.

QUESTIONS

1. In what areas of your life have you become hardened like a statue?

2. Jesus gives light to the darkest places of our souls. Even if you are ashamed of how you've acted in the past, give those dark places to God. Write down a prayer that surrenders your life's cold, dark parts to Jesus.

DAY 28
THE TRUE VINE

I am the vine; you are the branches. Whoever abides in me and I in him, he it is that bears much fruit, for apart from me you can do nothing. - John 15:5

If you've ever visited a vineyard, you can appreciate the beauty of a hillside covered with acres of grapevines. Some vineyards are hundreds of years old. The oldest grape-producing vine is located in Maribor in Slovenia. It is a Žametovka vine that has been producing fruit since the 17th century. I love the beauty of a vineyard; how a sunrise casts long shadows over the misty countryside covered in row after row of grapevines is captivating. The way a gardener can tame a wild vine is almost artistic. In a forest, vines are wild and grow wherever they please. However, when planted by a gardener, these vines grow in perfect lines and produce dozens of tons of grapes year after year.

Gardeners plant the seeds of a certain variety of grape, and that seed takes root and grows into another vine, and eventually produces the same variety of grape that was planted. When Jesus refers to Himself as the vine, He gives His disciples an image of what it means to be a disciple. He is teaching them what discipleship looks like. Much like growing a grape, the vine is rooted in the ground, and the vine sprouts branches each year. Then, these branches produce fruit that is good to eat or turn into wine, juice, or vinegar. The fruit can also be planted to produce more vines.

The fascinating part of this analogy is that when the seeds from the fruit are planted, they produce more vines, not more branches or fruit. If Jesus is the vine, and we are the branches, we will produce fruit that spreads the love of Jesus, not ourselves. Jesus' love produces more disciples, who produce more fruit, which spreads more of Himself. True discipleship does not replicate ourselves; it produces more of Jesus, and through His love and grace, Jesus grows more disciples.

If we, as branches, are not connected to Jesus, the vine, we are not connected to the life-source and therefore will not produce fruit. Just as Jesus says, "Apart from me you can do nothing." If we are trying to produce more of ourselves, we are not being effective disciples of Jesus. John 3:30 sums it up perfectly, "He must increase, but I must decrease." A disciple who produces more of himself has missed the point and has no place in God's vineyard. But a disciple who spreads the love of Jesus "bears much fruit."

As we explore this "I am" statement further over the next few days, let the prayer of Anabaptist elder Pilgram Marpeck, an Austrian engineer who was persecuted for his faith in the 1500s, be yours.

GARDENER GOD, YOU HAVE PLANTED AND PROTECTED US BY YOUR FAITHFUL HAND. SEND US THE SAP OF YOUR GRACE FROM CHRIST, THE TRUE VINE, AND MAKE US BLOSSOM AND BEAR THE FRUIT OF LOVE AS A SIGN OF YOUR LIFE IN US. LET THE SWEET FRAGRANCE OF THE SHOOTS YOU HAVE PLANTED GIVE YOU PRAISE FOREVER AND EVER.
AMEN.

DAY 29
THE TRUE VINE

When I would gather them, declares the LORD, there are no grapes on the vine, nor figs on the fig tree; even the leaves are withered, and what I gave them has passed away from them. - Jeremiah 8:13

Throughout this devotional book, we have seen Jesus undoing what Israel did to herself. These "I am" statements continue to show that Jesus came to rescue the world from the troubles that we brought upon ourselves. As we look at this "I am" statement, Jesus proclaimed He was the "true vine." It is important to look in the Old Testament at the promises of God for His people to understand this statement more fully.

When you read 1 Kings 4:25, 2 Kings 18:31, Isaiah 36:16, Micah 4:4, and Zechariah 3:10, a theme emerges where God's people were promised that they would live under their own vine and fig tree. What did this symbolize? Think about how the Israelites lived for so many years. They were in captivity in Egypt for 400 years. Then, they went from slaves in Egypt to a nomadic people who wandered in the desert for 40 years. And then, finally, they could establish a sense of place in the Promised Land. For the Israelites, an identity of place was important. They could plant crops, they could cultivate the land, they could grow a vineyard—something that takes time and care. Living under their own vine was a promise of peace, stability, and favor. And for many years, God allowed the Israelites to live in such a way.

However, as you can see in our key passage for today, because of Israel's disobedience and evil ways, God took away what He had given them. Once again, when Israel was in exile in Babylon, they were a nation without a sense of place. God stripped away their stability and favor, and their vines withered.

When Jesus proclaims that He is the true vine, He is stating that He will restore Israel in the eyes of God and that they would once again live under the protection and stability of the vine, which was Jesus. This vineyard would not be in a location but in the hearts of all who believe in Jesus, the true vine.

Israel often forgot who their true protector and provider was. They turned to idols and false teachings, and they were punished. If it weren't for Jesus and the grace of God, they would have no hope. As we look at Israel, it is easy to point the finger and look down on them for making such bad decisions. In reality, we are no different. We try to take matters into our own hands, turn to self-help methods, turn our backs on God, and mistreat others like Israel did. We are in just as much need of rescuing as they were. May we never be so prideful that we think we are immune to sin and evil. Praise God that His mercies never end.

QUESTIONS

1. In what ways have you tried to do things apart from God and failed?

2. What have you learned about depending on God as your provider and protector?

3. What does it look like to live under the true vine of Jesus?

DAY 30
THE TRUE VINE

I, the LORD, am its keeper; every moment I water it. Lest anyone punish it, I keep it night and day . . . In days to come Jacob shall take root, Israel shall blossom and put forth shoots and fill the whole world with fruit. - Isaiah 27:3, 6

Everyone wants to be part of a winning team. It happens every year: a team wins a championship, and their merchandise flies off the shelves. People buy hats, t-shirts, and vehicle decals for teams they had little interest in before their sudden rise to the top. Some people call this jumping on the bandwagon, but you can't fault people for this. It's human nature to want to be associated with success. But, if you are invested in a team and have followed and supported them for a long time, it's much more rewarding when your team succeeds.

When we look at the history of God's people, God has chosen to use the unlikeliest of situations to do the most extraordinary things. He chose an old man and woman in Abraham and Sarah to be the parents of a nation. He promised their descendants would be greater than the stars in the sky and the sands on the shore. From the beginning, God has promised victory. Even when all hope is lost, God provides a way. Isaiah 11:1 says, "There shall come forth a shoot from the stump of Jesse, and a branch from his roots shall bear fruit." God continues to make a way when there seems to be no way. God will always win.

When Isaiah promises that the world will be filled with the fruit from Israel, this is an eternal promise. So when Jesus said He was the true vine, He fulfilled these promises from Isaiah. He was the shoot from the stump of Jesse, and He was how the world would be filled with fruit. It would not happen because of an earthly kingdom and by force but a heavenly one that stretched far and wide for eternity. And it would happen through His followers sharing the love of Christ that lives in their hearts.

If you are in Christ, you are on the winning team. Even when things seem hopeless, and there seems to be no way out, God has made a way through Jesus. Don't lose heart.

QUESTIONS

1. When did God make a way for you when it looked like there was no way?

2. How did God show His faithfulness?

3. What does that teach you about future times when you may face hardships?

DAY 31
THE TRUE VINE

I am the true vine, and my Father is the vinedresser. Every branch in me that does not bear fruit he takes away, and every branch that does bear fruit he prunes, that it may bear more fruit. - John 15:1-2

I want to focus on the second part of this "I am" statement for our final devotional. Jesus said, "My Father is the vinedresser." That is a powerful image. I've learned to appreciate gardening through the years. As a gardener, I care for my plants, work the soil, feed the plants fertilizer, rid the garden of pests that could harm the plants, and enjoy the fruits of my labor. When I think of God as the gardener of the vineyard, I see Him as one who deeply cares for His vineyard. He is not passively working the vines. He is active, watchful, and intentional.

I've grown up around grape and muscadine vines. My grandfather grew them, my dad grew them, and even my father-in-law grows them. From my experience working with vines, the branches must be tended to in order to produce fruit. Branches that produce a lot of fruit get pruned each year, and they produce more fruit the next year. There are other branches, however, that only produce leaves and never produce fruit. Some people call these branches suckers. They suck the energy from the branches producing fruit, and they never amount to anything. A good gardener can identify these suckers because of their lack of fruit. They look lush and green, but they are harmful to the vine. These suckers are not pruned but cut back to the base of the vine so they will not continue to harm the rest of the plant.

When I think of God as the gardener, I think of Him as sovereign and good. He knows His vineyard and wants what is best for the entire countryside. He prunes branches that produce fruit and cuts off the ones that are harmful to the vine. And He is intentional with every step along the way so that the vineyard is the most fruitful it can be.

With Jesus as the vine and God as the gardener, our role is to abide in the vine and produce good fruit. How is that done? Well, you're doing a good job of it by finishing this devotional. By finishing this book, you have intentionally grown in your walk with Jesus. But your work is not done. We are not called to just absorb information about Jesus. We are called to make disciples.

Now that you have learned more about Jesus and His seven "I am" statements, what will you do with this knowledge? Use it to produce more fruit, spread Christ's love to others, and be confident in the Jesus you call Savior and the one who loves you. You will see that you are being fruitful when you feel that God is pruning you. When you feel like God is continually challenging you and trying to make you more in His image, that is God pruning you. Keep up the good work and abide in the true vine of Jesus, and you will produce much fruit.

ABOUT THE AUTHOR

Dr. Bryan Gill lives in Homewood, AL, with his wife and two children. He's an administrator and instructor in higher education and has written and contributed to a variety of books. Bryan enjoys all things outdoors with his family, including fly fishing, camping, and wildlife photography. He's also the co-host of The Storied Outdoors, a podcast somewhere between Lewis and Tolkien and Lewis and Clark. Learn more about Bryan and his other books at *www.bryangill.com*.

REFERENCES

1. Jeffrey E. Miller, "I Am Sayings," ed. John D. Barry et al., The Lexham Bible Dictionary (Bellingham, WA: Lexham Press, 2016).

2. *(https://www.worldvision.org/hunger-news-stories/world-hunger-facts)*

ironhillpress.com | 800.307.9366